RUSSIAN WARRIORS
Sukhois, MiGs and Tupolevs

RUSSIAN WARRIORS
Sukhois, MiGs and Tupolevs

R. Braybrook, S. Skrynnikov and L. Yakutin

OSPREY
AEROSPACE

Published in 1993 by Osprey Publishing
81 Fulham Road, London SW3 6RB

© Osprey Publishing

ISBN 1 85532 293 5

Edited by Tony Holmes
Page design by Bridgewater Design Ltd
Printed in China

Front cover Photographed in its natural
habit, the awesome MiG-31 *Foxhound* is
at its most potent cruising above the
strato cumulus. Capable of attaining an
altitude of 32,300 ft in under eight
minutes, the MiG-31 performs the vital
task of defending Russia's vast
boundaries from aerial intruders

Back cover Quintessential Cold War
warriors, these Tu-22 *Blinder B*s now
spend their time permanently grounded
at an engineering school on the outskirts
of Moscow. Still proudly wearing the air
force star on their fins, these stylish
machines will no doubt be sold for scrap
in the very near future

Title Page The small canards and
distinctive side-by-side cockpit
arrangement identify this aircraft as the
Su-27IB (Istrebitel-Bomardirovschik)
fighter-bomber, which made its quasi-
public debut at Machulische Air Base
near Minsk on 13 February 1992,
following a meeting of CIS defence
ministers. The Bureau have recently
denied the existence of any *Flanker*
derivative designated the Su-27IB,
calling this aircraft the KU instead. They
have claimed that this machine is a one-
off test airframe which might one day
serve as a fighter-bomber or carrier
trainer. At the moment it is unsuitable
for either role as it has no radar, folding
wings or arrestor hook. This aircraft also
differs from the standard Su-27 in having
twin nosewheels and no ventral fins. It
has been noted making practice
approaches to the carrier *Tbilisi*, but it is
assumed that this was purely aimed at
allowing naval pilots to evaluate the
merits of side-by-side seating

Right 'Red 31' is towed out for take-off
from its dispersal point, evidently by a
tanker that can top off its fuel capacity
before the pilot lights up the burners.
When the MiG-29 made its Western
debut in 1988, observers were staggered
to find that it had a higher thrust/weight
ratio than the F-16A. It was only when
the German Air Force inherited a batch
of MiG-29s after re-unification that the
West discovered that their remarkable
acceleration and climb rate had been
achieved at the expense of range and
endurance

For a catalogue of all books published by Osprey Aerospace
please write to:

**The Marketing Department, Reed Consumer Books,
1st Floor, Michelin House, 81 Fulham Road, London SW3 6RB**

Introduction

The thawing of the Cold War in the late 1980s, that preceded the disintegration of the Soviet Union into today's Commonwealth of Independent States (CIS), also served to raise the security curtain that had for decades surrounded combat aircraft in the East. The first manifestations of this new openness were the appearances of the MiG-29s at Farnborough in 1988 and the Su-27s at Le Bourget the following year.

This sudden relaxation of security was an eye-opener in several respects for long-time Western observers of the Soviet aerospace scene. For decades we had been brainwashed with the idea that designers on the other side of the Iron Curtain were basically plagiarists, and that their avionics and missiles were consistently a generation behind those at our disposal. In stark contrast to this belief, we learned that the Sukhoi and Mikoyan design bureaux were capable of highly original thought, that they were certainly willing to adopt ideas that had never been tested in the West, and that (in the case of the fourth postwar combat aircraft generation) they had gone to quite extraordinary lengths to perfect handling qualities.

It may be argued that this emphasis on flying characteristics was merely a reaction to the unsatisfactory safety record of the MiG-23/27 series, but the fact remains that Russian fighters are now being flown in a way that is simply not possible with their Western equivalents.

We also discovered in the late 1980s that the Soviets were ahead of us in the use of helmet-mounted sights and IRST (infra-red search and tracking systems) to augment the use of air intercept radars, and that they had developed special devices to protect their engines when operating from badly-surfaced (or bomb-damaged) runways. The Soviets had also shown considerable originality in facilitating the operation of the Su-25 from small dispersed sites, and their experience in Afghanistan had been put to good use in the protective measures fitted to that aircraft.

On the other hand, some of the traditional faults of Soviet aircraft remained. The MiG-29 was found to have a very short engine life, and it was clearly designed for a 'straight up, straight down' point defence sortie, which results in an outstanding thrust/weight ratio but very little fuel. In exporting their aircraft, it was found that the Russians had still not managed to develop satisfactory product support facilities.

Aside from discovering the remarkable qualities of their combat aircraft, we found that their designers were not only highly intelligent, but quite approachable, and willing to discuss their design philosophies in some detail. We saw that their test pilots were highly skilled, and we found they were just as great characters as their Western equivalents.

More recently, as the Russian economy has foundered, and all its citizens have become anxious to earn Western currency, we have discovered that their photographers are also fully capable of producing pictures to Western standards. After years of seeing uninformative, blurred reproductions in Soviet newspapers and magazines, this was just as great a surprise as the quality of the aircraft and of the people responsible for them.

The photographs selected by the editor for this book were chosen mainly for their sheer quality and information content. However, in covering many of the principal Russian combat aircraft types in service in the early 1990s they also provide a historical record of an air force (and to some extent the naval aviation service) at a critical time in its history. In the course of the next few years the present major cutbacks will continue, and many of the aircraft illustrated in these pages will undoubtedly be retired. These photographs may thus be regarded as a series of images of one of the world's greatest air forces when at its peak

Roy Braybrook
Ashtead, 1993.

Contents

Above The MiG-21 *Fishbed* series was undoubtedly one of the great combat aircraft designs, but there were so many sub-types that correct identification is not always possible. From OKB MiG drawings, the shape of the dorsal fairing suggests that this towed example is a MiG-21bis, but the mirror on the canopy indicates that it is more likely a well-weathered MiG-21SMT

Fourth Generation Fighters

Prior to the mid-1980s, Russian-designed fighters appeared in a series of quite distinct waves. They came at intervals of around ten years, and each generation represented an important advance in aviation technology. Thus, the first postwar generation appeared during the 1945-55 period, and were primarily characterised by swept wings and first-generation turbojets, many of which were basically copies of British engines. The second generation brought Mach 2 speeds, using afterburning axial flow turbojet engines in combination with very thin or highly swept wings.

The third generation retained this high performance, but employed variable-sweep wings to make possible operation from shorter airfields. Variable geometry also improved low-level penetration speed (and ride quality), and extended high-level loiter performance. Further advances in avionics, systems, beyond visual range (BVR) missiles, combat endurance and range were also apparent.

The fourth fighter generation that was to begin appearing in intelligence photographs in the mid-1970s might be regarded as an indirect response to America's experience in the Vietnam War. It had long been the US philosophy that technology was the key to success in aerial combat. The superior design of the F-86 (allied with the experience and rigorous training of the US pilots) over the MiG-15 had given a kill-ratio of 7:1 in Korea, and the Pentagon expected to see similar figures in any future conflict.

Left The interior of the front canopy of 'red 61' appears to differ from the Su-27UB shown to the West at Le Bourget in 1989 in having provisions for instrument flying training, with a blind and rails allowing the front cockpit to be blacked out as necessary. This photograph emphasises the enormous size of the world's largest air superiority fighter, and the immense stagger between the two cockpits

Control of the air had been taken for granted since the later years of World War 2, and technology was the way to achieve it. However, in Vietnam the technologically advanced F-4 had a hard time in maintaining an edge over the MiG-17 and MiG-21, and there were periods when the advantage tipped in favour of the North Vietnamese. The Phantom II had been built for BVR intercepts primarily, but the rules of engagement forced the Americans into close-in combat situations which neither USAF or USN crews had trained for. The North Vietnamese on the other hand had been instructed to fight according to the strengths of their aircraft, which meant dogfighting to survive.

Above Sukhoi Su-27UB 'red 63' is towed out to the business end of the runway, its radome still protected against the ravages of the Russian weather. One of many noteworthy features of the Su-27 is the great expanse of stainless steel around the gun, eloquent testimony to the power of this 30 mm cannon (and its muzzle flash), which is armed with 200 rounds of ammunition

Left Carrying an assortment of AA-10 *Alamo*s and AA-11 *Archer* air-to-air missiles under its wings and fuselage, a pristine Su-27 provides the backdrop as the flag of the Soviet Air Forces (Voyenno-Vozdushnyye Sily) is lowered at the end of the day

The unsatisfactory results achieved in South-East Asia encouraged the development of a new US fighter generation, the 'Teen-Series'. These aircraft would combine major advances in avionics and armament with a far greater emphasis on manoeuvrability, and a new generation of engines that allowed a very high aircraft thrust/weight ratio and an increased fuel fraction. Moreover, the F-4 would be replaced in the USAF not only by the ultimate in technology in the form of the F-15, but also by large numbers of highly agile F-16s. Whereas the F-4 was designed to shoot down nuclear bombers, the name of the game was now the aerial dogfight, and the USAF was out to win. BVR was not neglected by McDonell Douglas at the design phase however, the Eagle's large bulk being a result of the aircraft's fuel requirements for the intercept role.

Russian designers clearly faced an awesome challenge in attempting to develop fighters that could hold their own against America's forthcoming 'Teen-Series'.

Above Seen in side elevation, the Su-27UB displays the remarkable droop of the front fuselage, which evidently permits an excellent field of view from both cockpits for a drag penalty that this highly-powered fighter can tolerate, without a substantial performance penalty

Left The light of the setting sun serves to emphasise the elegant flowing lines of the Su-27, the air superiority fighter that brought Soviet combat aircraft abreast of their Western counterparts

Left The gentleman who appears to be listening intently to the pitot-static head of his Su-27UB is probably the back-seater, wearing his winter jacket over his standard-issue g-suit. His arm-badge seems to be some winged symbol, surrounded by the words Voyenno-Vozdushnyye Sily (Air Forces)

Right *Flanker* nosegear and groundcrew. The Russians have gone to great lengths to keep water, slush and snow thrown up by the nosewheel from interfering with operation of the engines, and this is evidenced by the sheer size of this mudguard. In the background, a fitter in winter gear shelters from the arctic wind and looks forward to a drop of something that will thaw his frozen bones

The key to this problem was to design a basic configuration that would allow operation to high angles of attack (AOA) without fear of departure from controlled flight, and without the engines surging. It has been claimed by some Sukhoi representatives that their bureau produced the basic design, with massive leading-edge extensions maintaining lift and directional stability to high AOA, and also directing the airflow into the two-dimensional intakes.

This configuration was tested in the tunnels of TsAGI (the Central Fluid Dynamics Institute in Moscow) and, according to the legend, it was there that members of the Mikoyan bureau were allowed access to it – there have been independent counter-claims that two MiG engineers designed the wing/forebody and took it with them to Sukhoi. The result was a smaller twin-engined fighter, the MiG-29, which is very similar to the Su-27 in basic shape, but in the F/A-18 size category, rather than that of the F-15

Above 'Shut those engines down before we both go deaf' The crew chief of 'red 10' exchanges a few last words with the gallant pilot before he blasts off. Note the massive combat camera, the head-up display, and the mirrors on the canopy arch. Also, on the side of the Su-27, the AOA sensor, and the damaged paintwork around the access panel screws, which denote outdated servicing procedures

Right Wide-angle rear-end shot of the Su-27UB, illustrating the nicely spaced engines and the Area-Ruled 'tail-sting', which provides a home for the braking parachute, radar-warning receiver and chaff/flare dispenser

Right Distorted unflatteringly by a wide-angle lens, 'red 07' and '15' are pictured at altitude in relatively clean configuration, their underwing pylons evidently a semi-permanent fit. The green fin areas and radome featured quite prominently on early *Flanker*s

Despite its somewhat larger size, the MiG-29 is in many respects the Russians' answer to the F-16; in simple terms, an aircraft that is employed in relatively large numbers and, although initially confined to PVO units in a defensive role, it is now not regarded as highly classified, which means it can be exported to most countries. The Su-27 is the Russians' top-of-the-range air superiority fighter, aimed squarely at the F-15.

From an operational standpoint, the MiG-29 has served as the MiG-21/-23 replacement in the tactical air superiority role (with secondary close air support/strike capabilities), and the Su-27 has taken over the responsibility of strategic interception from the Su-15 and the MiG-25. Both use new technology to meet new threats, and both provide their pilots with a far greater level of independence from ground-controlled intercept (GCI) stations than was previously available.

Left Photographed through a lens of more normal focal length, the Su-27 shows off its fine lines to much better effect. The emblem on the fin below the red star of the Communist Party is a stylised winged archer, this attractive design having been Sukhoi's bureau logo for many years following the cessation of World War 2

Sukhoi Su-27 *Flanker B*
Type: single-seat twin-engined all-weather fighter-interceptor
Dimensions: span 48.22 ft (14.700 m); length 71.95 ft (21.935 m)
Weights: normal TOW 48,500 lb (22,000 kg); max TOW 66,140 lb (30,000 kg)
Powerplant: two Lyulka AL-31F turbofans, each rated at 55,115 lb (25,000 kg) with afterburning
Armament: one built-in 30 mm GSh-301 single-barrel cannon, and up to 10 air-to-air missiles
Performance: max speed at altitude Mach 2.35 or 1345 knots (2500 kmh); max range 2160 nm (4000 km); service ceiling 59,000 ft (18,000 m); take-off run 1640 ft (500 m); landing run 1970 ft (600 m); max load factor 9g

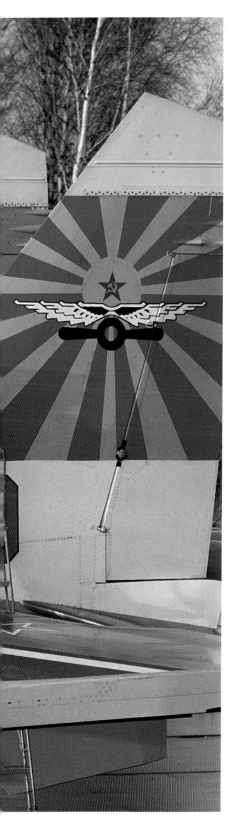

Above This Su-27 and Su-27UB are escorting a Tu-142K *Bear H*, the last production variant of this famous series. The Tu-142 differed from the Tu-95 basically in having an extended front fuselage, but this new-build cruise missile carrier reverted to the original length. It was developed to carry the AS-15 *Kent* missile, which is broadly equivalent to the USAF's AGM-86B

Left In stark contrast to the highly effective air superiority camouflage of the normal service aircraft, the Su-27s of the *Russian Knights* display team are painted in high-visibility colours, with the Air Forces' sunburst flag on the fin. The new Sukhoi logo is seen on the side of the intake duct, the winged helmet emblem being carried on the front fuselage. The team flies six aircraft, including at least two Su-27UBs. It is normally supported by an Il-76 *Candid* and is based at Kubinka AB, near Moscow

Above MiG-29 'blue 28' is about to be fitted with a large-calibre unguided rocket, hence the unusual pylon and shoe between the normal pylons for air-to-air weapons. The rocket appears to be very similar to the 240 mm S-240, but the stencilled markings appear to indicate that it is an S-245, suggesting a new development

Right An interesting study of Russian ground support equipment (GSE) as the projectile, evidently propelled by six separate rocket motors, is lifted off the ground prior to locating it under the wing. How this strange device can transfer it to the pylon shoe is not obvious

Left A last word with the crew chief before take-off. Noteworthy details include what appears to be an older type of 'bonedome' and the double reflectors of the HUD, giving an increased vertical field of view. The two stars painted on the fuselage might indicate two successful trials firings, or possibly that the pilot is a lieutenant-colonel (podpolkovnik)

Right Last minute eye-check for the trials pilot? The Russians appear to use only one size of helmet, with an inflatable liner to accommodate different head sizes. The visors are internal, possibly to allow the helmet-mounted sight to be clipped to the plate bonded to the front of the helmet. On ejecting, the liner is inflated by the emergency oxygen carried within the seat

Above The pilot seated in his MiG-29, with the internal visor down and oxygen mask in the extended position. The Russians have given a great deal of thought to safety equipment, as demonstrated by the dramatic escape of Anatoly Kvochur from his MiG-29 at Le Bourget in 1989, after an engine surged as he attempted to accelerate out of a slow-speed pass. His Zvezda K-39D ejection seat saved his life in a near-horizontal ejection at a height of about 300 ft (90 m)

Right A recent photograph of Mikoyan test pilot Pavel Vlasov standing beside the bureau's demonstration MiG-29UB, side-number 304. The white, blue and red stripe (ie, the Russian colours) was noted on this aircraft at the Berlin airshow (ILA-92) in June 1992. The reason for the large holes in the helmet is not clear, but they may be associated with the release of air during high-speed ejections

Above Engine checks for 'red 28' prior to starting take-off. Note the different afterburner diameters, suggesting that the left engine is being run up, while the right engine idles

Left The crew checks the pitot-static head (probably to see that the heater is working) prior to taxying out. Note the two non-standard middle pylons, presumably for RP trials, and the fact that the main intake doors are closed to prevent foreign object damage (FOD) to the engines while on the ground. When these doors are closed the engines take their air from auxiliary inlets over the wing, although this arrangement restricts internal fuel volume and has been discontinued on some later MiG-29 variants

Above A pleasing study of the MiG-29UB demonstrator, with the MiG-31 in the background at an unspecified airshow that evidently also featured the Su-27 family

Right Head-on view of the MiG-29UB with canopy raised. The two-seater, which retains the offset IRST of the MiG-29, features a massive periscopic device that improves the forward view from the rear cockpit on the approach

Above As 'blue 30' rolls in on the target in a medium dive attack, the RP under the starboard wing casts a broad shadow on the fuselage. The MiG-29 has a service clearance of 9.5g, although in airshows it is flown to 10.5g (Roman Taskaev is actually cleared to 11g!), a remarkably high figure in comparison with (for example) the 9g of the F-16

Left MiG-29 'red 48' heads out to the test-range with its large-calibre rockets. Only the Soviets developed such large unguided projectiles (which are approximately twice the diameter of the American HVAR), and it is difficult to envisage the type of target against which it would be used

Above The MiG-29M demonstrator, which made its Western debut at Farnborough in September 1992, is pictured here with two red X-31s, one 'AMRAAMSKI' and one R-73 (AA-11 *Archer*) under the starboard wing. The MiG-29M differs from earlier models in having a dorsal airbrake, a notched tailplane, four pylons per wing, uprated engines, and no overwing intakes. The main intake doors are replaced by grids similar to those used on the Su-27. The X-31s are supersonic ramjet-powered missiles for use against ships or radars

Left The RP streaks away from the trials aircraft, its exhaust nozzle glowing red. Such tests are used to confirm that the large volume of hot gases generated by the rocket do not cause the aircraft's engines to surge, and that the intense heat and acoustic vibration experienced by adjacent skinning during the first milliseconds of burn do not cause structural damage

Mikoyan MiG-29M *Fulcrum*
Type: single-seat twin-engined all-weather multi-role fighter-bomber
Dimensions: span 37.27 ft (11.36 m); length less nose probe 53.41 ft (16.280 m); overall length 56.82 ft (17.32 m)
Weights: normal TOW 33,000 lb (15,000 kg); max TOW 39,000 lb (18,000 kg)
Powerplant: two Leningrad RD-33K turbofans, each rated at 19,400 lb (8800 kg) with afterburning
Armament: one built-in GSh-301 single barrel 30 mm cannon, plus up to eight air-to-air or four air-to-surface missiles or up to 9920 lb (4500 kg) of bombs. Unspecified numbers of 80/130/240 mm unguided rockets
Performance: max speed at altitude over Mach 2.2 or 1260 knots (2335 kmh); max IAS permitted over 800 knots (1500 kmh); service ceiling 59,000 ft (18,000 m); max rate of climb 65,000 ft (330 m/sec); max range clean 1080 nm (2000 km), or 1725 nm (3200 km) with drop tanks; take-off run 820 ft (250 m); landing run 1970 ft (600 m); max load factor 9g

The Big MiGs

In one respect there is no doubt that the Russian Air Force is technologically in advance of any Western service, since its interceptors are capable of speeds approaching Mach 3. This capability has been provided for many years by the MiG-25 and its even more potent replacement, the MiG-31, which is now widely available for export.

The Mikoyan bureau began design work on this family in the late 1950s, evidently in response to intelligence reports regarding Lockheed work on the Mach 3 A-12 reconnaissance aircraft, which eventuated as the SR-71A, entering service in 1966. Whereas the US company developed a very sophisticated modified delta configuration, the Russians adopted a relatively conventional (by today's standards at least) fighter shape, with a moderately swept wing, Vigilante-style lateral intakes, and twin vertical tails.

From a structural design viewpoint, the main difficulty was to maintain strength and minimise distortion at the high temperatures produced by kinetic heating. Since the bureau felt that the large-scale use of titanium would prove to be prohibitively expensive and represent too much of a gamble, the airframe was largely designed in welded steel, which was to make up approximately 80 per cent of structure weight. A special high-temperature aluminium alloy forms a further 11 per cent, with titanium alloy representing only eight per cent. The remainder is presumably accounted for by the tyres, transparencies, etc.

In parallel with the interceptor, Mikoyan developed a high-altitude reconnaissance variant. There were three prototypes: the Ye-155P-1 interceptor and the Ye-155R-1 and R-3 reconnaissance aircraft. In the event the R-l flew first, on 6 March 1964, the fighter version flying on September 9th that year. Flight tests led to various modifications, notably wing anhedral to reduce dihedral effect, and the use of the tailplane to produce roll control at high airspeeds. The MiG-25P interceptor entered service in 1972, followed shortly afterwards by the MiG-25R reconnaissance aircraft and the MiG-25RB, which combined surveillance with a high-level bombing capability. The MiG-25BM 'Wild Weasel' defence-suppression aircraft was built in the early 1980s.

Left Easily distinguished from its big brother by its single mainwheels, this MiG-25 *Foxbat* provides an impressive show of afterburner combustion as its starts its take-off roll. The MiG-25PD continued to be manufactured until 1982 and remaining MiG-25Ps were modified to this *Foxbat E* standard. The aircraft is powered by 24,700 lb (11,200 kg) Mikulin-Tumansky R-15RB-300 turbojets

Above This rear view of a MiG-25 illustrates the massive diameter of the afterburners required to take this aircraft to Mach 2.83. The device mounted on the port outer pylon appears to be a dual launch rail for a lightweight missile such as the R-60 (AA-8 *Aphid*). These would be used in combination with the longer-range R-40 (AA-6 *Acrid*) missile inboard; the latter exists in both IR-homing (R-40T) and radar-guided (R-40R) forms

Left The setting sun emphasises the modified outline of the MiG-25PU *Foxbat C* trainer, in which the second cockpit (which is occupied by the instructor) was added ahead of the existing cockpit. This simplified structural changes, and was made possible by the fact that no operational equipment was required to be carried. The radar and all armament provisions are thus deleted

Mikoyan MiG-25PD *Foxbat E*
Type: single-seat twin-engined day/night all-weather interceptor
Dimensions: span 44.98 ft (14.015 m); length 64.80 ft (19.75 m)
Weights: Take-off weight (TOW) clean with full internal fuel 76,895 lb (34,920 kg); with four R-40 missiles 80,950 lb (36,720 kg)
Powerplant: two Mikulin-Tumansky R-15BD-300 afterburning turbojets, each rated at 19,400 lb (8800 kg) dry and 24,700 lb (11,200 kg) with afterburning
Armament: four R-40 (AA-6 *Acrid*) air-to-air missiles
Performance: max speed at altitude Mach 2.83 or 1620 knots (3000 kmh) available to 42,650 ft (13,000 m); max low-level speed Mach 0.98 or 647.5 knots (1200 kmh); time to 65,600 ft (20,000 m) and Mach 2.35 8.9 min; endurance 125 min; supersonic range on internal fuel 675 nm (1250 km); subsonic range on internal fuel 935 nm (1730 km); service ceiling 68,000 ft (20,700 m); take-off run 4100 ft (1250 m); landing run with parachute 2600 ft (800 m); max supersonic load factor 4.5g

The MiG-31 is a major derivative of the *Foxbat*, with more powerful Soloviev/Perm D-30F turbofans in place of the original Mikulin/Tumansky R-15BD-300 turbojets. The fuselage is stretched to allow for a second crew member, the wing is stiffened by the introduction of a third spar, and (to cope with increased take-off weights) the main undercarriage units are fitted with twin-wheels in a unique staggered arrangement. The aircraft's fuel capacity has been increased, and in later production aircraft a retractable probe is fitted just ahead of the windscreen to permit in-flight refuelling. The prototype Ye-155MP performed its maiden flight on 16 September 1975, and the MiG-31 entered service in 1983.

Above The NATO designation *Foxbat C* refers to both the MiG-25PU and the MiG-25RU, which provide conversion to the interceptor and reconnaissance variants respectively. In either case the maximum speed is reduced to Mach 2.65. One MiG-25PU was given the designation Ye-155 and was employed to make a series of women's' record flights (by Svetlana Savitskaya) during the late 1970s

Right The various dielectric panels and the optical window in the front fuselage indicate that 'white 40' is a variant of the MiG-25R, although it could be the -25RB with bombing capability. The latter was manufactured until 1982 in various sub-series (including the MiG-25RBK, RBS, RBV and RBT), differing only in terms of recce equipment and EW fit

Above Rear-quarter view of '374' prior to the Paris Airshow. The reasoning behind the twin mainwheels is that they make possible lower tyre pressures, and that the staggered arrangement avoids the deep ruts produced by a tandem (Viggen-type) configuration and the jamming of surface material between side-by-side wheels. The MiG-31 can thus operate from badly-surfaced airfields

Left Tarted up for its Western debut at Le Bourget in June 1991, the MiG-31 shows off its tandem clamshell canopies, unusually arranged twin mainwheels and the airbrakes under the intake ducts. Unlike the MiG-29 and Su-27, the MiG-31 has its IRTS mounted under the front fuselage in a retractable installation

Whereas the MiG 25 carries its main armament on four underwing pylons, the MiG-31 can carry four AA-9 long-range air-to-air missiles under the fuselage, in addition to lighter weapons on the wings. The later aircraft also has a GSh-23-6 Gatling gun mounted on the starboard centre fuselage, the weapon being located in this position presumably to eliminate engine surging due to gunfire. The MiG-31 is claimed to have the world's first electronically-scanned radar, and a data-link that allows four aircraft flying in line-abreast to sweep an area 430 to 485 nm (800-900 km) wide. The radar can track ten targets and engage four of them simultaneously.

Although both the MiG-25 and the -31 are restricted to a maximum speed at altitude of Mach 2.83, giving a ground speed of 1620 knots (3000 kmh), they are substantially faster than the Mach 2.50 F-15, and they can hold their maximum speed for longer than the few seconds of the USAF fighter. These 'Big MiGs' are truly remarkable aircraft.

Above Seen in flight, the MiG-31 demonstrator has a certain powerful beauty. However, very few airshow visitors saw it fly at Le Bourget since it seldom got off the ground due to poor serviceability, although it was scheduled to fly each day

Right Checking out *Foxhound*. The groundcrew in the foreground appear to be running tests on the nose-mounted sensor. The transport in the background is an Antonov An-72/74 *Coaler*

Left MiG-31 'blue 02' is towed into the line-up. The fact that the aircraft has only two underwing pylons suggests that it does not represent the later production standard, which added a further pair of hardpoints. The original idea was that the main armament of four fuselage-mounted AA-9 *Amos* would be supplemented by two AA-6 *Acrid*s or four AA-8 *Aphid*s on the two wing pylons. The bureau also cleared a ferry configuration, with a large ventral tank and two AA-8s for self-defence

Mikoyan MiG-31 *Foxhound*
Type: two-seat twin-engined day/night all-weather interceptor
Dimensions: span 44.17 ft (13.464 m); length 74.43 ft (22.688 m)
Weights: TOW with full internal fuel (armament not specified) 90,390 lb (41,000 kg); with two 550 Imp gal (2500 litre) external tanks 101,850 lb (46,200 kg)
Powerplant: two Perm D-30F6 afterburning turbofans, each rated at 20,950 lb (9500 kg) dry and 34,170 lb (15,500 kg) with afterburning
Armament: one GSh-23-6 six-barrel 23 mm cannon with 260 rounds, plus four AA-9 *Amos* missiles under fuselage, plus four AA-8 *Aphid*s or two AA-6 *Acrid*s under wings
Performance: max speed at altitude Mach 2.83 or 1620 knots (3000 kmh) available to 57,400 ft (17,500 m); max low-level speed Mach 1.22 or 810 knots (1500 km/hr); time to 32,800 ft (10,000 m) 7.9 min; max endurance 3.6 hr with external tanks, or up to seven hours with flight refuelling; ferry range 1620 nm (3000 km); interception radius with four AA-9s, using Mach 2.35 cruise, 390 nm (720 km), or 755 nm (1400 km) using Mach 0.85 cruise and two external tanks, increasing to 1190 nm (2200 km) with in-flight refuelling; take-off run at max TOW 3950 ft (1200 m); landing run 2600 ft (800 m); service ceiling 67,600 ft (20,600 m); max supersonic load factor 5.0g

Above MiG-31 'blue 33' is towed out past a line of Su-15 *Flagon*s, the furthest of which appears to be an Su-15U *Flagon G*, a two-seat conversion aircraft that retains an operational capability. Next to it sits a single-seat *Flagon F*. It is believed that around 1000 Su-15s were built, but that many were replaced in the air defence role by the MiG-25. It was an Su-15 that shot down the Korean Air Boeing 747 (flight KL007) over Sakhalin Island while it was en route from Anchorage to Seoul on 1 September 1983

Previous page A reminder that the MiG-31 serves in some inhospitable areas, this photograph also illustrates the more sophisticated flying gear required for high altitudes, especially in regard to the full-pressure helmet. The multi-prong antenna just ahead of the windscreen provides IFF facilities, and the small dielectric fairing on the intake lip presumably serves as a radar-warning receiver

Left No built-in steps with this 'baby'. The radar-operator evidently has to stand on the intake to gain access to the rear cockpit. The green padding on the hood probably serves to minimise heat transfer, rather than to avoid the crew knocking themselves out in turbulence

Left The two crew members exchange a last crack. The canopies obviously have to be jettisoned prior to ejection, and there are powerful actuators on either side to ensure that these heavy structures really do depart. The seats in such aircraft employ some lateral dispersion for safety. Note the periscope and its actuator on the rear hood

Right The pilot ensconced in his K-36D seat. The cylindrical devices just over his shoulders house the telescopic rods that deploy the drogue chutes to stabilise the seat. In conjunction with the appropriate flying suit and helmet, the K-36D can provide safe escape up to 82,000 ft (25,000 m) and speeds up to Mach 3. In high altitude ejections the main chute is not deployed until the seat is down to 16,400 ft (5000 m)

Above The MiG-31 taxies out with the periscope raised. The purpose of this device is not obvious, since it appears to be fitted to all aircraft of this type. It may simply be used to allow the back-seater to assist the pilot during night and bad weather approaches

Right Periscope down, flaps at about 40 degrees, and full afterburner. The starboard main undercarriage is just leaving the runway, the bogie beam inclined for stowage. The use of flaps for take-off varies between fighter types, many using a zero setting, and others using flaps only to reduce unstick speeds at high weights

Strike

In the early post-war years the Soviet emphasis was on designing point-defence interceptors to defend key targets against the threat of the nuclear bomber. To achieve a high climb rate and an excellent ceiling, they had high thrust/weight ratios and moderate wing loadings, which also made them useful dogfighting aircraft, though of limited endurance. Despite the reliance placed on the Ilyushin Il-2 *Shturmovik* during World War 2, close support appears to have been given a relatively low priority. Such duties were fulfilled by obsolescent interceptors with something less than outstanding success.

This philosophy continued for a long time, the MiG-17 being superseded in the ground attack role by the MiG-21, which (like its predecessor) was more remarkable for its ability to defend itself than for its payload-radius performance. The Soviets' first useful jet-powered ground attack aircraft was probably the Sukhoi Su-7, which with a variable sweep wing and uprated engine became the Su-17. With an even more powerful engine and various refinements, this progressed to the Su-17M *Fitter K* (designated the Su-22 for export) series, which represented a major improvement over the MiG-21 in this role. They could 'bomb along' at very high speed at sea level without shaking the pilot's teeth loose, and they were built to last, which is an important attribute in the worst possible fatigue environment.

In parallel with the Su-17/22 family, the Mikoyan bureau developed the MiG-23/27 series. This proved to be outstanding in terms of multi-role potential, and was effectively a poor man's F-4. In the case of the MiG-23, the primary role is air defence, hence variable-geometry multi-shock intakes are used to provide the highest possible maximum speed. For the MiG-27 the primary role is ground attack, hence lightweight fixed pitot intakes suffice. The two variants are distinguished by their intakes, not by the nose shape. Both have underfins that rotate to the horizontal for take-off and landing and the MiG-27 has another unusual feature in the form of bomb pylons under the rear fuselage, which suggests an automatic pitch-trim change on weapons release.

Right This appears to be an Su-24MK *Fencer D*-mod on tow, photographed in 1990. The use of a tanker for towing purposes is standard practice. This version of the Su-24 differs from the standard *Fencer D* in lacking the massive wing fences just inboard of the hinge, extending back over the upper surface

Above Like many other Sukhoi aircraft, this *Fencer C* proudly wears the distinctive archer logo on its nose

Left This rear-quarter view illustrates the size of the vertical tail and the parachute fairing at its base. The merits of variable-sweep wings have long been debated, but there is no doubt that this feature facilitates ground handling and accommodation in hardened aircraft shelters (HAS)

Sukhoi Su-24M *Fencer D*

Type: two-seat twin-engined variable sweep strike aircraft
Dimensions: max span 57.87 ft (17.64 m); min span 34.01 ft (10.366 m); length 80.48 ft (24.532 m)
Weight: TOW 87,633 lb (39,750 kg)
Powerplant (estimated): two Lyulka AL-21F3A turbojets, each rated at 24,700 lbs (11,200 kg) with afterburning
Armament: single built-in cannon of unspecified type. Guided weapons are listed as H-23M (AS-7 *Kerry*), H-25 (AS-10 *Karen*), H-28 (AS-9 *Kyle*), H-29L/T (AS-14 *Kedge*), H-59T (AS-13 *Kingbolt*), H-58 (AS-11 *Kilter*) and R-60 (AA-8 *Aphid*). Guided or unguided bombs in the range 110 to 3300 lbs (50 to 1500 kg) can be carried, as can unguided rockets in the series S-5, S-8, S-24 and S-25
Performance: max speed at low level Mach 1.14 or 755 knots (1400 kmh); max speed above 3300 ft (1000 m) 865 knots (1600 kmh); range clean 755 nm (1400 km); range with two PTB-3000 tanks 1540 nm (2850 km); take-off run 4250 ft (1300 m); landing run 3300 ft (1000 m)

Left The weapons systems officer, wearing the latest headgear with internal visors, works through his pre-flight checklist prior to strapping in. With this level of protection, the K-36D ejection seat provides safe escape up to speeds as high as Mach 2.5 and 700 knots (1300 kmh)

At the upper end of the tactical strike spectrum, the Su-24 is broadly comparable to the F-111, but the Russian aircraft has a much higher thrust/weight ratio, and presumably a much smaller radius of action. The first version entered service in 1974 amid considerable secrecy; according to official sources, the aircraft did not deploy outside the Soviet Union until 1979, when some aircraft were sent to an airfield near Berlin.

As it happened, the first public showing of this series in the West was to take place not far away, at Berlin-Schönefeld in June 1992, when an Su-24M *Fencer D* appeared at the ILA-92 airshow. Three months later a tactical reconnaissance version, the Su-24MR *Fencer E* was exhibited at Farnborough, with a brand-new equipment fit that was claimed to have both civil and military applications. Further export sales are thus being sought, in addition to the existing deliveries to Libya and Iraq (and thus to Iran) and a reported sale to Syria. Despite its age, the Su-24 remains one of the world's most potent strike aircraft, and in the wrong hands could represent a very serious threat.

Right More orange tubular GSE, on this occasion to transport braking parachutes to the aircraft. If the antenna at the top of the rudder serves a radar-warning receiver, then it may be that the small radome over the parachute fairing is a missile approach warning device

Above The two crew members of the Su-24 sit side-by-side in rather cramped accommodation, wearing somewhat old fashioned headgear. The stencils on the levers on the massive central beam, OTKP and 3AKP, are presumably abbreviated forms of 'open' and 'locked' respectively. The construction number 2615304 appears to be typical of seven-digit identifications for this series

Right Another example of obsolescent head-gear, worn by a young pilot who may have to start shaving soon. Strapping oneself into the aircraft and making all the connections is evidently a lengthy process. The modern K-36 seat has a lever on the right side of the seat-pan that can be used to apply extra tension to the various straps

Right Illustrating the unusual hood arrangement of the Su-24, this shot also denotes a transitional phase in safety equipment, with the pilot wearing a modern helmet and the weapon systems officer still sporting the older pattern. This lacked the inflatable liner, and was presumably far less comfortable

Above Russian ground attack aircraft appear to have no standard paint scheme. In this case the upper surfaces of green, brown and tan are combined with a light grey undersurface, the distinctive shades being separated by a straight demarcation line

Right A well camouflaged MiG-23 taxies past a line-up of similar aircraft and a high-visibility control tower at some unknown airfield. The aircraft currently make an ideal strafing target, but in wartime they would retire to the earth-covered shelters seen in the background

Right Pressure refuelling is carried out via a receptacle just aft of the port main undercarriage bay. One of the disadvantages of a variable sweep design is that it almost inevitably leads to a fuselage-mounted undercarriage, with a relatively narrow track and a complex retraction geometry

Far right Installing the braking parachute on the *Flogger* is clearly a much lighter task than in the case of the *Fencer*. The array of fin-mounted rear warning devices appears to be common to all *Flogger*s. The parachute deploys in a double-cruciform configuration

Previous page All heavy maintenance naturally takes place under cover. Possibly due to the low standards of their groundcrew conscripts, the Soviets went to great lengths to develop automatic test equipment that could identify faults in all the aircraft systems. Some of this ATE is clearly in use here

Above Some air forces use mechanical loading devices, but muscle-power is quicker. In this case an R-23 AA-7 *Apex* is being placed on the launch-rail under the fixed glove of the variable-sweep wing on a MiG-23. This type of aircraft is frequently seen with one radar-guided R-23R and an IR-homing R-23T, sometimes augmented by a pair of R-60s (AA-8 *Aphid*s) under the fuselage

Left A reminder of the range of pilot sizes that the cockpit designer has to allow for; two officers head for their MiG-23UB, a type illustrated by the aircraft on the right. For many years the nose number colours denoted the aircraft's unit allegiance, the inside shade indicating its division, and the border its squadron. This system has now been discontinued

Above This looks like a variation on the old joke about the Canadian salute following unification of the three services, but he is supposed to be striking his forehead with a clenched fist. In reality, the instructor is probably just using his hands as fighter pilots always have, to illustrate a manoeuvre

Left With his R-23 missile on the fixed glove, all the pilot of MiG-23 'white 06' needs is a clipboard to remind him of the markings used by the USAF and the Republic of Korea Air Force. Could this be some kind of aggressor training?

Right A MiG-23UB being prepared for tow, the narrow lines connected to the mainwheel units suggesting that it may be possible to apply the brakes externally. Yet another camouflage scheme is used, with the fin evidently painted tan and brown

Above A final check on those traditionally bald Russian tyres before 'white 07' taxies out to join his buddies. Note the rear-view mirror and the triangular IFF antenna just ahead of the windscreen. The NATO-standard coat-hook marking indicates a hoist-point

Left Close-up of the front fuselage. It seems likely that the cruciform canopy framework is unique to the MiG-23UB, being associated with the use of a curtain over the front cockpit for instrument training

Above The MiG-23MLD on tow, illustrating the effectiveness of the camouflage scheme when seen against natural vegetation. The longitudinal strakes just ahead of the afterburner nozzle are stiffeners for the airbrakes, of which this series has four, their symmetrical disposition above and below the fuselage datum probably eliminating pitch change on extension and retraction

Left The massive leading edge extensions and notched glove indicate that this is a MiG-23MLD *Flogger K*, which also features variable-sweep outer pylons and a smaller ventral fin

Mikoyan MiG-23ML *Flogger G*
Type: single-seat single-engined fighter-bomber
Dimensions: max span 45.82 ft (13.965 m); min span 25.52 ft (7.779 m); fuselage length less nose probe 51.61 ft (15.73 m)
Weights: normal TOW 34,720 lb (15,750 kg); max combat TOW 40,565 lb (18,400 kg); max ferry TOW 45,570 lb (20,670 kg)
Powerplant: single Tumansky/Khatchatourov R-29-300 turbojet, rated at 27,560 lb (12,500 kg) with afterburning
Armament: one 23 mm GSh-23L twin-barrel cannon plus typical air-to-air armament of four R-60 (AA-8 *Aphid*) and two R-23R/T (AA-7 *Apex*) missiles. Typical air-to-ground armament S-8 rockets in B-8 pods or S-5 rockets in UB-32 pods, or S-24 rockets
Performance: max speed at altitude Mach 2.35 or 1350 knots (2500 kmh); max IAS with 16° sweep 430 knots (800 kmh); max IAS with 45° sweep 650 knots (1200 kmh); max IAS with 71° sweep 755 knots (1400 kmh); service ceiling 60,700 ft (18,500 m); max range clean 1050 nm (1950 km); max range with three 174 Imp gal (790 litre) tanks 1520 nm

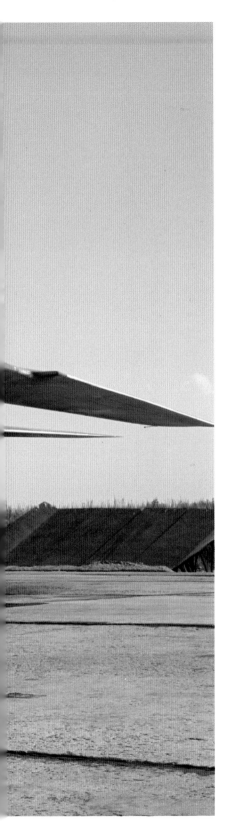

Above A MiG-23UB *Flogger* C prepares for take-off, the two suction relief doors in the side of the intake duct opening as the 22,050 lb (10,000 kg) R-27F2M-300 engine accelerates. The 'UB' designation indicates Uchebniy Boevoy, or combat trainer. As with other early production MiG-23s, fuel tanks appear to be carried under the outer wing only during ferry sorties. The wing is then restricted to the 16-degree sweep position, although in an emergency the tanks can be jettisoned complete with their pylons

Left The MiG-27M *Flogger* J is a very late production version of this fighter-bomber, distinguished from earlier models by the wing leading edge extension along the fuselage and the arrangement of sensors on the nose. One interesting feature of the series is the "scabbed on" armour by the cockpit, where 'yellow 2' is painted

Left The clearest possible illustration of the distinctive *Flogger J* nose, with a radar ranger above the laser ranger, the pitot-static head relatively high on the starboard side, and the 'Swift Rod' ILS antenna on the port side. There is a slightly later variant, known to NATO as the J2, in which the pitot head is set lower and the small radome projects much further

Far left *Flogger J* in flight, showing how a good camouflage scheme can be spoiled by the glint of metal from the after-burner and the white of the pilot's helmet. The MiG-27M differs from the preceding MiG-27D in its equipment fit, which includes the more advanced 'Fone' laser in place of the earlier 'Klem'

Above It is regrettable that the photographer provided no information on this picture, since there is not sufficient airframe visible to identify this particular Su-17 *Fitter*, and the garb of the character on the left suggests some special trial. The weapon being loaded clearly has flip-out fins, and its slight taper at the rear end suggests it may well be powered. Since the nose cannot be seen, it is impossible to say if it is guided

Left This shot of 'yellow 21' is a good illustration of the ventral fin in the extended position. Designers are attracted by ventral fins because they retain their effectiveness at high AOA, whereas dorsal fins are adversely affected by the reduced dynamic pressure and vortices created by the fuselage and intakes. However, any sizeable ventral fin has to be folded horizontally for landing, take-off and ground operations

Left This immaculate aircraft appears to be a MiG-21bis *Fishbed L* in ferry configuration, with two of the large supersonic external fuel tanks mounted under the outer wings to supplement the standard centre-line tank. Compared to earlier models, the MiG-21bis is distinguished by its enlarged spine, housing considerably more fuel, but it also has a more powerful engine, modernised avionics, and an airframe with a longer fatigue life

Bombers

Whereas the honours in fighter development were equally shared between the Mikoyan and Sukhoi design bureaus, the bomber field has virtually been a Tupolev monopoly, with Ilyushin and Myasishchev squeezed out at a relatively early stage. The first post-war generation of Soviet bombers consisted of the Tu-4 *Bull* (a copied B-29), which was developed into the Tu-70/-85, and from which the twin-jet Tu-16 *Badger*, the four-jet M-4 *Bison* and the remarkable Tu-95 *Bear* (the world's only swept-wing aircraft with turboprop engines) evolved. Although something of an oddball, the Tu-95 manages to combine long range and endurance with a reasonably high cruise speed. These qualities have made it especially useful in maritime patrol and strike duties, and it is still rolling off the production line today, optimized primarily for the former role.

The Myasishchev M-4 was clearly designed for nuclear strikes against North America. However, it is believed that its range proved inadequate, and that most M-4s were converted to tanker duties, or handed over to Naval Aviation for use in maritime reconnaissance.

The Tu-16 is a much lighter aircraft, presumably intended for use in the European theatre. It is broadly comparable to Britain's Valiant and America's B-47, both of which it has outlasted by a considerable margin. Most early Tu-16s were adapted for the aerial refuelling role, but subsequent models have been employed in maritime patrol and anti-shipping strike, electronic intelligence (ELINT) and electronic warfare (EW) duties. The Tu-16 was also built in China as the H 6.

In attempting to develop a supersonic long-range bomber, the Soviets first tried the M-50 *Bounder*, a massive delta-configuration aircraft with four engines mounted on the wings. However, this failed to progress beyond the prototype stage, and the Myasishchev bureau was closed down in 1960. The Soviets' first successful supersonic bomber was the Tu-22 *Blinder*, which replaced the Tu-16 in the intermediate-range bombing role. It combined a moderately swept wing with two afterburning engines mounted in pods over the rear fuselage. The design appears to have relied to a large extent on the use of Area Rule to minimise transonic wave drag as it accelerated up to a maximum speed of around Mach 1.4. Although the Tu-22 was successful in

Right A Tu-160 *Blackjack* with its wings spread and flaps down, main bogies turning round and nose gear already stored, begins to clean up its launch configuration following rotation. Noteworthy features include the full-span leading-edge flaps and the very high proportion of the trailing edge devoted to flaps. The main undercarriage design, with each leg carrying six wheels on three axles, is very unusual

Left The crew of the Tu-160 prepare to change their peaked hats for modern 'bonedomes'. Even on the latest of Russian bombers, the traditional bomb-aimer's window is retained, although the crew presumably now look through it using video equipment

Right This front-quarter view illustrates the careful blending of the thick wing roots into the fuselage, and the use of a fixed stub at the base of each tailplane-half to minimise leakage

Tupolev Tu-160 *Blackjack*
Type: four-seat, four-engined variable-sweep strategic bomber
Dimensions: max span 182 ft (55.5 m); length 177 ft (54 m)
Weights: max TOW 606,000 lb (275,000 kg)
Powerplant: four Samara/Trud NK-321 turbofans, each rated at 55,115 lb (25,000 kg) with afterburning
Armament: six AS-15 *Kent* or 12 SRAM-type missiles on rotary launcher, or approx 36,000 lb (16,500 kg) of conventional bombs
Performance: max speed at altitude Mach 2.07 or 1185 knots (2200 kmh); radius of action 3950 nm (7300 km) (all data approximate)

Above The full crew of four, evidently walking away from a successful landing. The crew gains access to the cabin by means of a hatch in the top of the nosewheel bay and a corridor running forwards between the avionics bays

Right More engineering details of the Tu-160, the most interesting feature being the all-moving upper fin, which moves as a slab for yaw control. The moving part of the wing appears to be a good fit within the fixed glove, and there are large dielectric areas on the leading edge of the fixed fin. What appears to be a long, narrow stainless steel member along the side of the rear fuselage may simply be an external stiffener

Left Generations apart, the Tu-160 flies in echelon port behind the aged Tu-16, representing a gap of almost 30 years in terms of first flight dates. Seen in highly swept configuration, the *Blackjack* shows its use of spoilers and the outboard flap section for lateral control, and the way that an area of wing is raised vertically as it is swept back, presumably to minimise intrusion into the fixed glove. The purpose of the fairings over the wing roots is not immediately obvious

achieving a supersonic dash speed, it was quickly relegated to reconnaissance, EW and maritime strike duties.

In restricting production of the Tu-22, the Soviets probably felt that the introduction of a variable-sweep wing would improve the speed range and subsonic cruise performance, and that a substantially heavier aircraft was required to combine good warload-radius performance with a supersonic dash. However, it was also decided to abandon the podded engine installation, and bury the powerplants in an enlarged fuselage.

Above A rare photograph of an AS-4 *Kitchen* air-to-surface missile, which the Russians call 'Burya', being attached to the starboard glove pylon of a Tu-22M *Backfire*. The series was originally armed with a single AS-4 semi-buried under the centre fuselage, but two underwing launch shoes were later added

Right This frontal view of a Tu-22M3 *Backfire C* carrying two AS-4s demonstrates the massive wetted area that was accepted in developing this aircraft from the Tu-22 with its podded engines. However, that broad fuselage is also indicative of long range, since fuel presumably fills the space between the engines. This variant is distinguished from its predecessors by the use of Vigilante-type intakes

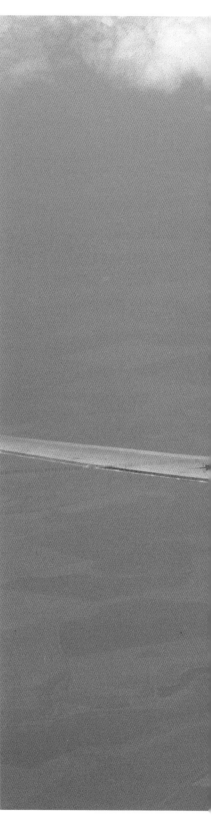

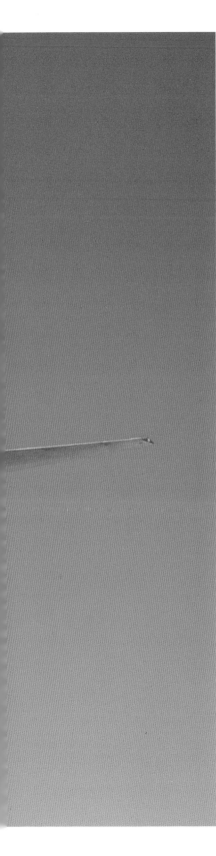

Above An attractive study of two Tu-22M3s armed with AS-4s. It is believed that this missile exists in two forms: a strategic strike version with a 200 kT nuclear warhead, and an anti-ship version with a conventional warhead

Left This excellent illustration of the Tu-22M3 shows the AS-4 in two different forms, one with a conventional forward-looking radome and the other with a downward-looking dielectric panel, possibly suggesting a medium altitude cruise. The Tu-22M3 made its Western debut at Farnborough in 1992, but mounted practice bomb carriers rather than AS-4 pylons

Tupolev Tu-22M3 *Backfire C*
Type: four-seat, twin-engined variable-sweep medium bomber
Dimensions: max span 112.5 ft (34.3 m); min span 76.75 ft (23.4 m); overall length 130 ft (39.6 m)
Weights: max TOW 273,370 lb (124,000 kg)
Powerplant (estimated): two Kuznetsov NK-144 turbofans, each rated at 44,100 lb (20,000 kg)
Armament: normal warload one X-22 (AS-4 *Kitchen*) or 26,450 lb (12,000 kg) of bombs; max warload three X-22s or 52,900 lb (24,000 kg) of bombs. One flexibly-mounted 23 mm GSh-23 twin-barrel cannon in tail turret
Performance: max speed at altitude Mach 1.88 or 1080 knots (2000 kmh); combat radius 1080 nm (2000 km); service ceiling 43,600 ft (13,300 m); take-off speed 200 knots (370 kmh); take-off run 6560 to 6900 ft (2000 to 2100 m); normal landing speed 154 knots (285 kmh); normal landing run 3950 to 4250 ft (1200 to 1300 m)

Left One of the advantages of dealing with large engines is that access to the front compressor stages to inspect for blade damage is far easier than in the case of a fighter. We have recently become accustomed to seeing the lower edge of an intake flattened to minimise FOD, but why Tupolev chose to flatten the top of the Tu-16 intake is probably lost to posterity

Right Surely one of the largest gate-guards in the world, this Tu-16 retains the glazed nose and pilot-operated NR-23 cannon of the original *Badger A*, but has a thimble nose radome and other changes. The stylised aircraft and Pentagon on the nosewheel door is a unit efficiency award

Below Another derivative of *Badger A*, this Tu-16 appears in natural metal finish, with a different set of additions to the front fuselage. Despite its age, the Tu-16 is still employed by the Soviet Air Forces and Naval Aviation for reconnaissance, EW and ELINT duties

Left Not an operation to perform in a high wind! Noteworthy points include the substantial guards to prevent leg-flailing on ejection, and the relatively large size of Russian construction numbers in comparison with modern practice. Their size may reflect the fact that when the Tu-16 was built, photographers were rarely allowed this close

Below left Start of the ejection seat loading sequence, as the seat is raised from its trolley by another piece of tubular GSE. The Tu-16 was broadly equivalent to the British V-bombers, which used both ejection seats and conventional escape measures

Right One might guess that this is the engineering officer signing to certify that the ejection seats have been correctly installed. Soviet uniforms vary according to the service, the time of year and the occasion. Without sight of collar tabs and shoulder boards, it is impossible to identify rank

Left An interesting example of 'Mae West' design, modelled by this Tu-16 crew member. Note the aircraft's thimble radome and auxiliary fuel tanks

Far left The navigator comes up from the nose of the Tu-16 for a conference. The flying gear contrasts strongly with that currently used in both fighters and bombers, especially in regard to the helmets

The result was the Tu-22M *Backfire*, which, despite its designation, appears to have been a completely new design, though doubtless benefiting from the Tu-22 experience. There are thought to be around 400 Tu-22Ms in service, of which perhaps a third are with Naval Aviation.

With confidence inspired by the Tu-22M, and with Soviet Strategic Aviation demanding something to equal the Rockwell B-1, Tupolev designed the four-engined Tu-160 *Blackjack*, which attained operational status in the late 1980s. The Tu-160 is, in fact, somewhat heavier than the B-1B, and is capable of Mach 2.07, whereas the USAF aircraft is limited to Mach 1.25. Given suitable systems and weapons, the Tu-160 may be a highly effective strategic bomber.

Left The pilot in charge straps in to his ejection seat and fastens on his helmet. The complexity of strapping-in procedures has long been a sore point, since the crew member needs one set of straps to connect him to his parachute, and another set to restrain him to the seat

Below left Another member of the crew, probably a gunner. The remotely-controlled barbettes of the Tu-16 were inspired by those of the Tu-4 *Bull*, virtually a copy of the B-29

Right A picturesque but unnamed base, and a Tu-16 with nosewheels off the ground. In the background are some camouflaged Mi-26 *Halo*s and An-26 *Curl* transports

Tupolev Tu-16 *Badger*

Type: twin-engined medium bomber with six-man crew

Dimensions: span 108.04 ft (32.93 m); length 114.2 ft (34.8 m)

Weights: empty 84,950 lb (38,530 kg); max TOW 167,100 lb (75,800 kg)

Powerplant: two Mikulin AM-3M non-afterburning turbojets, each rated at 21,000 lbs (9500 kg)

Armament: typical missile armament two AS-2 *Kipper*s, AS-6 *Kingfish* or AS-5 *Kelt*s. Defensive armament up to seven NR-23 23 mm cannon in three barbettes and a single-gun fixed nose installation

Performance: max cruise speed Mach 0.74 or 424 knots (786 kmh); radius of action 970 nm (1800 km); service ceiling 39,360 ft (12,000 m); ferry range 2320 nm (4300 km); max endurance 5 hr 40 min

(Weights and performance figures relate to Chinese B-6D)

Above In the air the Tu-16 is a reasonably handsome aeroplane. Its twin 23 mm tail guns are turned safely upwards, and it appears to be trailing a long HF antenna for long-range communications

Above right The start of the world's strangest flight refuelling operation. The tanker is trailing a hose from the starboard wingtip, and this is clearly venting fuel

Below right A rare close-up of the Tu-16N's wingtip, the aircraft probably being a modified *Badger A*. The hose is evidently extended through a metal tube rigidly attached to the wingtip

Above Line-up of Tu-22 *Blinder*s in storage, the white areas indicating protective covers. The Tu-22 represented the Soviets' first supersonic bomber, but was soon superseded in production by the much heavier Tu-22M

Right The receiver aircraft (fitted with the strange fairing over the left windscreen) formates with the tanker, the hose being stabilised by means of a small parachute

Tupolev Tu-22 *Blinder B*
Type: three-seat, twin-engined medium bomber
Dimensions: span 92 ft (28.0 m); length less probe 133 ft (40.5 m)
Weights: max TOW 190,000 lb (86,000 kg)
Powerplant: two Koliesov VD-7F turbojets, each rated at 30,900 lb (14,000 kg) with afterburning
Armament: single AS-4 *Kitchen*. Defensive armament unspecified 23 mm cannon in tail turret
Performance: max speed at altitude Mach 1.4 or 800 knots (1485 kmh); radius of action 1025 nm (1900 km)
(All data estimated)

Above The first evidence in this series of photographs that women are employed in engineering functions. The colour of the clothing is in line with groundcrew overalls, but the scarf strikes an informal note, possibly suggesting that she is a representative of one of the equipment manufacturers

Left The high-mounted engines of the Tu-22 demand equally lofty servicing platforms, but access may be easier than in the case of the buried engines of the Tu-22M. The four-wheel bogie retracts aft into trailing-edge fairings which, if well designed, may actually reduce the compressibility effects on the wing

Right Judging by the clouds of vapour, this Tu-22 is being given a top-up of liquid oxygen. The tubular tower in the background illustrates the inconvenience associated with high-mounted engines

Below right As in the cases of the M-50 *Bounder* and the first F-104s, the ejection seats of the Tu-22 are fired downward to eliminate the problem of clearing the vertical tail, though with the disadvantage that such seats cannot be used at low-level. In this photograph one of the three seats is being winched up into the cockpit

They also serve

Fighters and bombers are attention-grabbers in the sense that their design pushes technology to the limit, and that they actually deliver the explosives that hopefully win the fight. However, these combat aircraft clearly represent only a fraction of a service's total inventory. There are many other types of aircraft that are technically interesting and are equally vital to the conduct of operations.

One area in which the Soviets have been able to hold their own is the rotary-wing field, in which they can claim both the heaviest and the fastest products in the world. The best-known name in this field is probably Mil, a bureau that has developed a wide range of land-based helicopters, including the Mi-24 *Hind* assault aircraft and the more recent Mi-28 *Havoc* attack design.

However, in the shipboard context the Kamov series dominates the scene, their contra-rotating main rotors providing advantages both on deck and in the hangar, due to their smaller diameter and the absence of a tail rotor. These naval helicopters have gone through four generations, starting with the little two-seat Ka-15, which was followed by the much more useful Ka-26 *Hoodlum*, the turbine-powered Ka-25K *Hormone*, and more recently the Ka-29 *Helix B*. The bureau's latest product is the Ka-50 *Hokum*, which beat the Mi-28 in the Russian Army contest for a new attack helicopter, and is being marketed in the West under the name Werewolf.

The Soviets have also been very successful in the development of amphibians, a field monopolised for decades by the Beriev design bureau. The most important in numerical terms is the Be-12 Tchaika turboprop, of which around 100 were built, and which is now being developed as a water-bomber. Beriev (strictly speaking, the Taganrog Aviation Scientific and Indsutrial Complex) has now received a production order for the twin-jet Be-42 Mermaid anti-submarine warfare aircraft, the prototype of which made its Western debut at Le Bourget in 1991.

Right Although Kamov helicopters with their distinctive contra-rotating rotors are traditionally associated with shipboard operation, they are also operated from land bases. This example, which is about to clear the snow from a large area, appears to be a Ka-27 *Helix A*

Transport aircraft are of crucial importance in a modern war. This category has largely been dominated by the Antonov series from Kiev in the Ukraine, while Ilyushin (based in Moscow) concentrated more on commercial airliners. However, the A-50 *Candid* is employed in both civil and military forms, and has provided the basis for an interesting series of developments, modifying the aircraft for other roles.

Top The Be-12 taxies out for its patrol mission. The rectangular section of the two stores suggests some form of dispenser, and the starboard outer pylon appears to be missing. There is believed to be an internal weapons bay just aft of the step in the hull

Above As the winter sun lights up the mountain in the background, a Be-12 is prepared for flight. Its engines are set high to minimise corrosion from salt water, and the levels of spray are reduced by the strake over the bow

Left The Beriev Be-12 Tchaika (Seagull) first flew in 1960, and is used in anti-submarine and maritime patrol duties in association with the Northern and Black Sea fleets

The two principal derivatives are, in fact, the Il-76 (*Mainstay*) airborne warning and control system, which has a radome over the rear fuselage, and the Il-78M *Midas* tanker. The Il-78M made its Western debut at Farnborough in 1992, equipped with three hose-and-drogue refuelling units.

No review of Soviet aircraft would be complete without mention of the name of Yakovlev, a bureau that is currently more concerned with civil products, but has also provided the CIS Navy with a transonic V/STOL aircraft, the Yak-38 *Forger* and the Yak-141 *Freestyle*, which could become the world's first supersonic V/STOL aircraft to enter service.

Above Aerial refuelling is used to extend range of large aircraft in strike and mariti patrol missions, its application to tactical aircraft being a relatively new developme the CIS services. In this unusual plan-vie photograph an Il-78M refuels a Tu-142 fro hose-drogue unit attached to its port rear fuselage. The Il-78M carries two addition pods under the outer wing panels

Left Servicing any aircraft outdoors in winter adds all kinds of problems, and the Be-12 is probably no exception. In this pleasing composition the petals of the port engine are opened for access, and the MAD sting in the tail is just visible

Right Wide-angle view, showing the observation windows and the relatively small sea-search radome in the nose. The Be-12's sensors include a MAD (magnetic anomaly detection) sting extending aft from the rear fuselage

Following pages Night-time operating techniques are rarely illustrated, but this photograph appears to show the use of truck-mounted searchlights to illuminate a landing zone for helicopters, in this case the Mi-26 *Halo*

Beriev Be-12 Tchaika (Seagull) (NATO: *Mail*)
Type: twin turboprop amphibian with crew of five, for ASW and maritime patrol duties
Dimensions: span 97.47 ft (29.71 m); length 98.99 ft (30.17 m)
Weights: max TOW 68,345 lb (31,000 kg)
Powerplant: two Ivchenko AI-20D turboprops, each rated at 4200 shp
Armament: unpublished weight of torpedoes, mines and depth charges
Performance: max cruise speed 328 knots (608 kmh); normal cruise speed 172 knots (320 kmh); max rate of climb 3000 ft/min (15.25 m/sec); max range 4050 nm (7500 km)

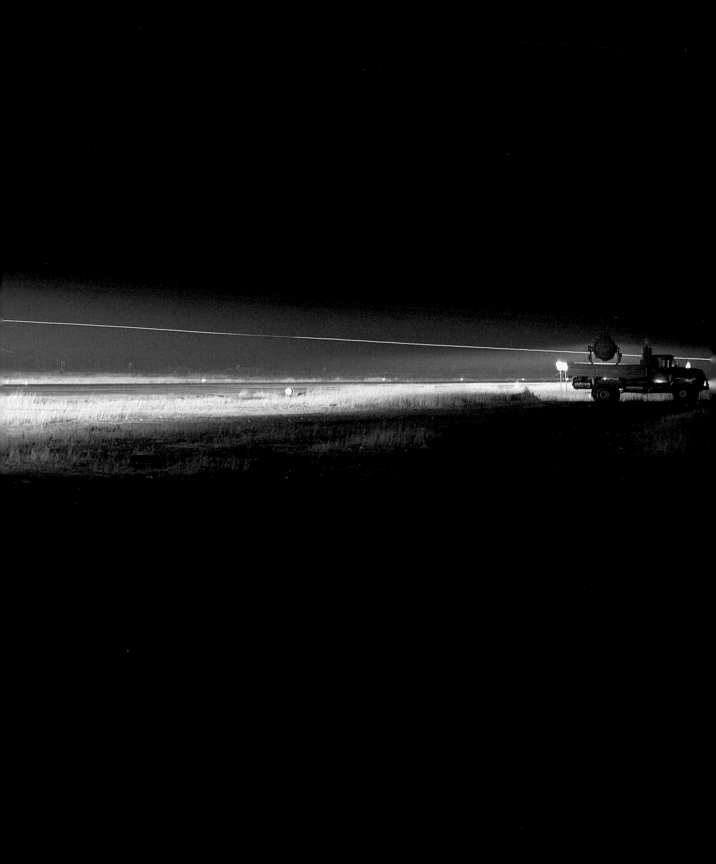

Naval Aviation

Britain is dedicated to the use of V/STOL aircraft in providing fixed-wing air power from ships at sea, since it significantly reduces the cost of the carrier. The US Navy accepts the advantages that V/STOL provides for the Marine Corps in its amphibious operations, and may adopt V/STOL in replacing the F/A-18, presumably because it will increase the number of fighter-capable ships.

The Soviets have carried out extensive service trials with the Yak-38 V/STOL aircraft, and funded the initial development of the supersonic Yak-141 in order to keep the naval V/STOL option open. However, their development of high-powered conventional fighters with outstanding control characteristics at low speeds offered the prospect that they could take off from carriers without requiring catapults, provided that a ski-jump was installed at the bow. Such aircraft would still need arrester gears, but at least the catapult problem would be eliminated.

In order to test this concept, a series of deck trials were carried out, beginning in late 1989, from the 'aircraft-carrying cruiser' *Tbilisi*, later renamed the *Admiral Nikolai Kuznetsov*. These involved modified variants of the MiG-29, Su-25 and Su-27, and they appear to have been generally successful, discouraging further work on the Yak-141.

However, in view of the CIS nations' funding problems, it remains to be seen how much effort will be poured into creating seaborne aviation that might one day rival that of America. It currently appears that the second of the class (*Varyag*, formerly *Riga*) may be sold to China or India, possibly with navalised Su-27s or MiG-29s, but no-one can decide who actually owns it, and there is an impasse over how it will be completed. At the moment it is just a bare shell; the third (*Ulyanovsk*) will be scrapped. The future is thus uncertain.

Right This aircraft is the second MiG-29K built by Mikoyan, and the vessel on which it is standing is the carrier *Tbilisi* now renamed *Kuznetsov*. The pilot is the legendary Roman Taskaev, who was responsible for performing many of the arrestor landings marked up on the aircraft's side

Left The MiG-29K is about to touch down on the *Tbilisi*, cruising past the Su-25UTG (the G stands for 'Gak', which means 'hook' in Russian) and the Su-27K parked out of the way behind the island. Note the hook and periscope of the Su-25UTG, and the foreplane and R-73 (AA-11 *Archer*) missile of the Su-27K

Right No notes have been provided by the photographer regarding the identity of the two aircrew, but the striped T-shirt of the officer on the right may indicate that he is with Naval Aviation. The aircraft in the background is clearly some form of Su-27 .

Below right A handsome portrait of the *Tbilisi*, with an Su-25 *Frogfoot* about to leave the angled deck, and a Ka-27 parked abreast of the island. The 67,000-ton *Tbilisi* was laid down in 1983, launched in 1985, and began sea trials in 1989. Broadly comparable in size to the recently retired *Midway* (CV-41) class carriers, this vessel was intended to be the first of a series of three, of which the last (*Ulyanovsk*) was to have a greater displacement at around 75,000 tons

Above The Su-25UTG begins its take-off run along the flat angled deck. The basic Su-25UT made its Western debut at Le Bourget in 1989, and is essentially an unarmed version of the Su-25UB *Frogfoot B*, which is employed for pilot conversion and FAC duties, and is distinguished by its hook. The Su-25UTG adds a stronger hook to the -25UT, and local strengthening appropriate for carrier landings. Reports indicate that five Su-25UTGs were built for these trials, and that an order was later placed for five more

Below right The Su-25UTG and Su-27K are prepared for take-off, while a Ka-27 shipguard hovers in the background. The Su-25UTG appears to be standing on the aft deck-edge lift, the other elevator being situated on the same side, ahead of the island. The curved deck-line is indicative of the distortion produced by the wide-angle lens. Note the foreplane and drooped leading edge of the Su-27K, the radome of which appears to have suffered damage from hailstones

Sukhoi Su-25 *Frogfoot B*
Type: single-seat, twin-engined close support aircraft
Dimensions: span 47.11 ft (14.36 m); overall length 50.95 ft (15.53 m)
Weights: normal TOW 32,187 lb (14,600 kg); max TOW 38,800 lb (17,600 kg)
Powerplant: two non-afterburning Tumansky R-195 turbojets, each rated at 19,840 lb (9000 kg)
Armament: fixed 30 mm twin-barrel cannon with 250 rounds, plus a normal ordnance load of 3100 lb (1400 kg) or a max load of 9700 lb (4400 kg) on eight underwing pylons. Two AA-8 *Aphid*s can be carried on the outer pylons for self-defence
Performance: max low-level speed 526 knots (975 kmh); max range with two droptanks and combat load 400 nm (750 km) in LO-LO profile or 675 nm (1250 km) HI-LO-HI; service ceiling 23,000 ft (7000 m); take-off or landing run 2000 ft (600 m); max load factor 6.5g with normal load, reducing to 5.2g with max load

Right The Su-27K makes its unassisted take-off from the ski-jump, demonstrating that a high-powered fighter with very effective low-speed controls can benefit from V/STOL developments, without accepting the penalties associated with jet lift. In pioneering this technique the Soviets have opened the way to operating high performance combat aircraft from ships that have no catapults, which may prove an important development in naval air warfare

Right The Su-27K is taxied to one of the take-off positions at the bottom of the ski-jump. The deck markings indicate two possible lines for such take-offs, at the start of which the aircraft is restrained by retractable plates in front of the mainwheels, while it runs up to full afterburning thrust, the jets being deflected by large hinged plates raised from the deck. Such take-offs are spectacular, but weight is presumably very limited

Following page An excellent photograph of the MiG-29K, illustrating the wing fold, single enlarged dorsal airbrake (replacing the rear-end clamshells), and the notched leading edge for the tailplane. The wingtips have been thickened, reportedly to accommodate RWR antennas. With the deletion of the overwing intakes, additional fuel is carried in the wings. Aside from the normal navalisation changes (arrester hook and stronger landing gear), the aircraft has been given a new radome shape for its NO-10 radar, two extra underwing pylons, a retractable flight refuelling probe and uprated RD-33K engines

Above Mikoyan test pilot Roman Taskaev appears to be taking along his own device for canopy fragmentation, should the jettison system fail. Taskaev is well known in the West for his MiG-29 airshow demonstrations

Top Judging by the amount of gold braid on his hat, this could be the ship's captain, warning the pilot that he may have to swim back to shore if he dents his brand-new carrier!